STEM IN THE REAL WORLD

METEOROLOGY
IN THE REAL WORLD

by Gregory Vogt

Content Consultant
Lourdes B. Avilés
Professor of Meteorology
Plymouth State University

Core Library

An Imprint of Abdo Publishing
abdopublishing.com

abdopublishing.com

Published by Abdo Publishing, a division of ABDO, PO Box 398166, Minneapolis, Minnesota 55439. Copyright © 2017 by Abdo Consulting Group, Inc. International copyrights reserved in all countries. No part of this book may be reproduced in any form without written permission from the publisher. Core Library™ is a trademark and logo of Abdo Publishing.

Printed in the United States of America, North Mankato, Minnesota
082016
012017

THIS BOOK CONTAINS
RECYCLED MATERIALS

Cover Photo: Jens Büttner/Picture-Alliance/DPA/AP Images
Interior Photos: Jens Büttner/Picture-Alliance/DPA/AP Images, 1; NASA GSFC/Science Source, 4; Staff/MCT/Newscom, 7 (left), 7 (middle), 7 (right); NASA, 10, 35, 37, 43; Everett Historical/Shutterstock Images, 12; Shutterstock Images, 16; NOAA, 19, 45; Ken McKay/ITV/Rex Features Images, 22; John Bazemore/AP Images, 26; US Air Force, 29; Lynne Sladky/AP Images, 30; Science Stock Photography/Science Source, 32; Red Line Editorial, 39; Jim Reed/Science Source, 40

Editor: Arnold Ringstad
Series Designer: Ryan Gale

Publisher's Cataloging-in-Publication Data

Names: Vogt, Gregory, author.
Title: Meteorology in the real world / by Gregory Vogt.
Description: Minneapolis, MN : Abdo Publishing, 2017. | Series: STEM in the real
    world | Includes bibliographical references and index.
Identifiers: LCCN 2016945469 | ISBN 9781680784824 (lib. bdg.) |
    ISBN 9781680798678 (ebook)
Subjects: LCSH: Meteorology--Juvenile literature. | Climatology--Juvenile
    literature.
Classification: DDC 551.5--dc23
LC record available at http://lccn.loc.gov/2016945469

CONTENTS

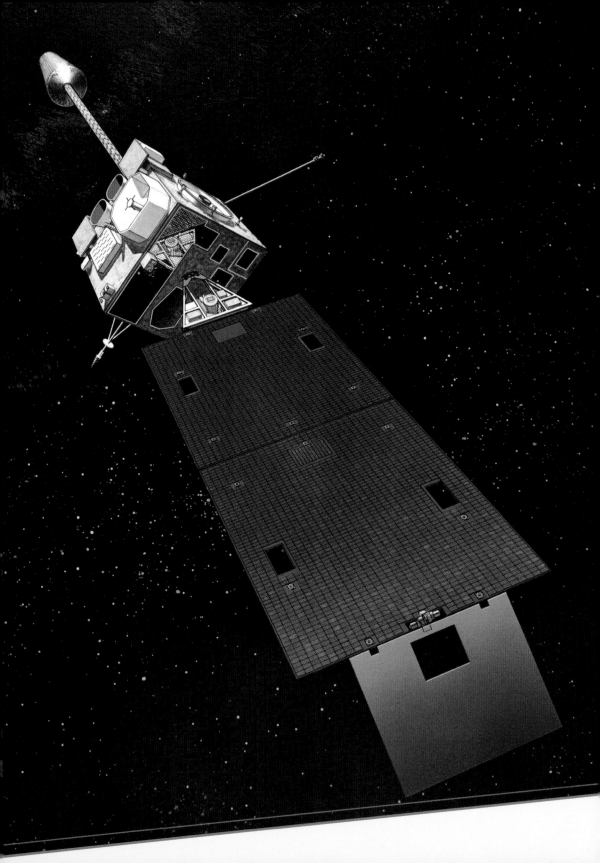

A HURRICANE NAMED SANDY

High above the equator, a group of satellites circles Earth every 24 hours. They orbit Earth at the same speed the planet rotates. This means each satellite stays directly above a point on the ground. They are called geostationary operational environmental satellites (GOES). In 2016 three of these satellites were active. They observe

Satellites are critical tools for US weather forecasting.

weather patterns in the western hemisphere from an altitude of 22,236 miles (35,785 km).

On October 22, 2012, one of the GOES saw a disturbance over the Caribbean Sea. Swirls of clouds appeared south of Kingston, Jamaica. Meteorologists took notice. They watched the swirls grow and strengthen. The swirls became a storm. The storm was soon named Tropical Storm Sandy.

Sandy moved northward. It crossed Jamaica and Cuba and grew into a hurricane. The meteorologists used computer programs to predict Hurricane Sandy's

IN THE REAL WORLD

GOES

The GOES system monitors Earth's weather. Scientists, engineers, and technicians design and build the satellites. Other teams use rockets to launch the satellites into space. Technicians control the satellites and collect their pictures and data. Meteorologists study the pictures and data to create weather forecasts. The first of these satellites was launched in October 1975. As new ones are launched, old ones are shut off.

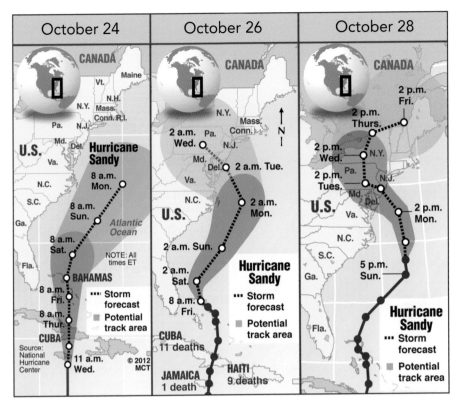

| October 24 | October 26 | October 28 |

The Path of Hurricane Sandy

Computers predicted many possible paths Hurricane Sandy could follow. The predictions shifted as the storm moved and scientists collected more data. It was hoped that the storm would remain over the Atlantic Ocean and then dissipate. Instead, Sandy crossed over land. These maps show predictions of the storm's path on October 24, 26, and 28. How did the predictions change as time went on?

course. They determined the storm would likely strike land near New Jersey around October 29. Sandy continued to strengthen as it moved across the ocean. It slammed into the New Jersey coast right on schedule.

Early forecasts of Sandy's path gave people along the coastline time to prepare. They protected their homes and stocked up on supplies. Emergency responders got ready for the storm. In many places, local governments ordered citizens to evacuate. They wanted people to wait out the storm in safer places.

In spite of the preparation, Hurricane Sandy killed more than 200 people. A total of 106 of them were Americans. The other fatalities occurred in island countries, including Haiti, Cuba, and Jamaica. Sandy caused more than $50 billion in damage. More than 650,000 homes were damaged or destroyed. Millions of people lost electrical power. Sandy was a terrible disaster. It highlights the importance of studying hurricanes and other dangerous weather events.

Meteorology: A Vital Service

Meteorology is the scientific study of Earth's atmosphere. This is the layer of gas, water, and dust surrounding the planet's surface. Meteorologists study the atmosphere for many reasons. One of these reasons is weather forecasting. People want to know what their day will be like. They want to know whether it will be rainy, sunny, hot, or cold. They want to know if dangerous weather conditions, such as lightning, tornadoes, or hurricanes, are on the way.

Meteorologists study the atmosphere in many ways. They conduct laboratory experiments to learn how gases behave and interact. They go outside and use instruments to measure air conditions. These

Weather and Climate

Weather is what is happening in the atmosphere right now. It may be hot or cold, dry or rainy. Climate is different. In places where it rains often, the climate is rainy. In places where it is dry most of the time, it may be a desert climate. The difference between weather and climate is time. Weather is what happens over a short period. Climate is how the atmosphere behaves over a long period. Understanding the climate helps forecasters make long-term weather predictions.

Weather satellites capture detailed pictures of Earth's clouds.

instruments measure temperature, wind, moisture, and sunlight. Some instruments fly in airplanes or on satellites such as GOES. Satellite photos of clouds can tell meteorologists the direction the air is moving.

Every day meteorologists collect weather data on the ground, in the air, and in space. Their goal is to figure out what is happening in our atmosphere. They use this information to predict what will happen next. The atmosphere is one of the most complex systems scientists study. Today's meteorologists are working hard to understand it better. Weather forecasting has saved many lives. Improved predictions of dangerous weather could save even more.

FURTHER EVIDENCE

Chapter One discusses the work of meteorologists. What was one of the main points of this chapter? What evidence was used to support that point? Read the article at the website below. Does the information on the website support the main point of the chapter? Does it present new evidence?

How Do Meteorologists Predict the Weather?

mycorelibrary.com/meteorology

CHAPTER TWO

THE SCIENCE OF THE ATMOSPHERE

Benjamin Franklin was an American scientist and inventor. He lived in the 1700s. One of his interests was watching the weather. He studied clouds and weather conditions. He was especially interested in storms. He discovered that lightning is electricity. He invented lightning rods to protect homes during thunderstorms. These metal rods are placed above the roofs of buildings.

Franklin is said to have flown a kite in a thunderstorm to study lightning and electricity.

They attract lighting so the electricity safely travels to the ground rather than damaging the building. Franklin was one of the first American meteorologists. But he did not invent meteorology. The study of weather goes much further back in history.

People began forecasting weather more than 2,600 years ago. The Babylonians, who lived in what is now Iraq, forecasted weather by observing clouds. Chinese astronomers studied the weather to make calendars. The ancient Greek philosopher Aristotle wrote a book called *Meteorologica*.

The Lunar Eclipse of 1743

Benjamin Franklin was prepared to watch a lunar eclipse in 1743. But a storm clouded the skies of Philadelphia, Pennsylvania, where Franklin lived. Franklin later learned that people in Boston, Massachusetts, could see the eclipse. For them, the same storm arrived hours later. This observation led Franklin to try to explain how storms moved. Franklin guessed that the atmosphere has areas of high pressure and low pressure. The different pressures caused the air to move.

Aristotle explained clouds, wind, rain, and hail. He also had explanations for thunder and lightning. He never tested his ideas about weather. Some of his ideas were correct, but scientists now know many of them were wrong.

The Birth of Weather Instruments

For centuries, collecting weather data meant just looking at the sky. People watched clouds and felt the weather. They tried forecasting what would happen next. When should they plant crops? Was it safe to venture far from shore in boats? Would winter be long?

Some weather knowledge was turned into common sayings. One was "Red sky at night, sailors' delight. Red sky in the morning, sailors take warning." A red sky at sunset meant a storm had already passed. A red sunrise meant a storm was coming. Sometimes these sayings held true, but not always. Basic observations were not enough. Early meteorologists

Before the age of modern meteorology, people used simple observations, such as the color of the sky, to guess the weather.

began inventing tools to help them observe and predict the weather.

The first weather instruments were simple. German philosopher Nicholas of Cusa lived in the 1400s. He discovered a method of estimating humidity. He hung a piece of wool outside. He found that the wool was heavier on damp days than on dry days. His invention was not very useful, but it was a start.

Italian scientist Galileo Galilei worked in the 1500s and 1600s. He discovered that gases and liquids expand when heated. This led to the invention of the first thermometers. Air or liquid inside the thermometers expanded when warm and contracted when cool. These changes showed whether the air temperature was rising or falling.

Another Italian scientist, Evangelista Torricelli, created the first barometer in the 1600s. Barometers measure air pressure. Because Earth's atmosphere is always moving, pressure changes

IN THE REAL WORLD

Temperature Scales

Today, two temperature scales are commonly used. Daniel Fahrenheit invented the Fahrenheit scale in 1724. Anders Celsius developed his own scale in 1742. It was later revised and named the Celsius scale in his honor. Water freezes at 32 degrees Fahrenheit and boils at 212 degrees. Water freezes at 0 degrees Celsius and boils at 100 degrees. Meteorologists in the United States usually report temperature in Fahrenheit. In most other countries, the Celsius scale is used.

from day to day. Pressure changes indicate changes in the weather.

Many other weather instruments followed. Rain gauges measure how much rain has fallen. Devices called anemometers measure wind speed. Other devices measure the moisture in the air.

Using their instruments, meteorologists began collecting real data. They recorded data and compared it with their other observations. Still, something important was missing. Weather does not happen over only one spot. What happens in one place affects what happens in another. Meteorologists from different locations needed to share data. But messages could take days or weeks to arrive. This was much too long to be useful.

Creating Modern Meteorology

In the 1830s and 1840s, Samuel Morse and others developed the electric telegraph. Telegraphs sent messages over long distances instantly. Weather data could be shared with faraway locations. Soon a

Scientists at the US Weather Bureau prepare a forecast in the 1920s.

network of telegraph wires stretched across the countryside.

Meteorologists began sending weather data to the Smithsonian Institution in Washington, DC. By 1870 the United States had created a national weather service. Its purpose was to coordinate weather reports. The weather service began forecasting the weather. It was later reorganized into the US Weather Bureau.

The invention of the radio in the 1890s changed everything again. Weather data and forecasts could be received anywhere. This became especially important to ships at sea. Storm warnings enabled captains to navigate safer routes. By the 1920s, people could communicate with voice rather than radio clicks.

Weather instruments improved rapidly. Scientists in airplanes started measuring the upper atmosphere. Weather instruments were lofted with helium balloons. By the mid-1950s, radar began mapping areas where it was raining. A few years later, the first weather satellites were launched. They took pictures of clouds from high above the planet. Then computers began processing weather data.

Meteorologists now have incredible tools. Forecasts have improved greatly. Predictions of severe storms save many lives. But in spite of new technologies, forecasts are still not 100 percent accurate. There is still much to be learned about the atmosphere and its weather.

Benjamin Franklin was a great watcher of the weather. He took particular interest in understanding lightning. In his own words, Franklin talks about weather systems that produce lightning:

> When there is great heat on the land in a particular region . . . the lower air is rarefied, and rises; the cooler denser air above descends; the clouds in that air meet from all sides, and join over the heated place; and if some are electrified, others not, lightning and thunder succeed, and showers fall. Hence, thunder-gusts after heats, and cool air after gusts; the water and the clouds that bring it coming from a higher and therefore a cooler region.

> As electrified clouds pass over a country, high hills and high trees, lofty towers, spires, masts of ships, chimneys, as so many prominences and points draw the electrical fire, and the whole cloud discharges there. Dangerous, therefore, is it to take shelter under a tree during a thunder-gust. It has been fatal to many, both men and beasts.

Source: Benjamin Franklin. *"Experiments and Observations on Electricity."* Smithsonian Libraries. *Smithsonian, n.d. Web. Accessed June 27, 2016.*

What's the Big Idea?

Benjamin Franklin wrote about his discoveries regarding lightning in the passage above. What are his main ideas about storms and lightning?

Risk
of
shower

Heavy
rain

Clear
&
dry

CHAPTER THREE

CAREERS IN WEATHER SCIENCE

People around the world forecast the weather every day. If there are low, gray clouds in the sky, it is a good guess that a storm is coming. This is a simple weather forecast. Meteorologists observe the sky too. But they also use the power of science and technology to create their forecasts.

Forecasters on television help warn the public about dangerous weather conditions.

To the public, the most visible meteorologists are those on television. Just about every television news station has its own weather forecaster. These people may or may not have a degree in weather science. Many have studied meteorology in college. Their job involves presenting weather information to the public.

Television weather forecasting is only one meteorology career. There are many others available. The public does not usually hear much about these careers. But they are essential and lifesaving.

Many meteorologists work for the National Weather Service (NWS). This is a US government agency. It is a part of the National Oceanic and Atmospheric Administration (NOAA). Scientists in the NWS have many different jobs. Some collect weather data and create the local forecasts that television meteorologists use. Some study satellite pictures and track weather systems. Others do basic research. They may study how climate change is affecting weather patterns.

Some meteorologists work with powerful computers. They write programs for collecting and analyzing weather data. Other meteorologists design weather satellites. Research meteorologists may travel to places such as Antarctica and Greenland. They sample the ice, because ice contains pockets of air from long ago. Studying this ancient air helps them learn about the history of the atmosphere.

IN THE REAL WORLD

Private Weather Forecasting

The NWS updates its forecasts every few hours. These are available for anyone to use. Many businesses, however, get special forecasts from private companies. The construction, transportation, energy, and agriculture industries pay for forecasts. For example, power companies want to know if hot spells are coming. They will need to produce more electricity for air-conditioning. Farmers want to know if it will rain. This can tell them if they will need to turn on watering systems for their crops. Many private weather companies provide these special forecasts.

A US Air Force crew flies into Hurricane Wilma in 2005.

Studying Storms

The Air Force Reserve Weather Reconnaissance
Squadron flies large aircraft into hurricanes. Inside
the storm, meteorologists measure wind speed
and direction. They drop weather instruments into
the storm. As the instruments fall, they measure air
temperature, pressure, and wind speeds. The data is
radioed to meteorologists so they can predict how the
storm will develop.

There are other kinds of storm chasers. States such as Oklahoma, Kansas, and Nebraska experience some of the most violent storms. The storms produce tornadoes. These funnels of wind rip across the land. They shred anything in their path. Tornado storm chasers design instruments to measure and film tornadoes. When a tornado develops, the chasers race in their vehicles to get ahead of it. They deploy their instruments and then leave as fast as they can.

Measuring tornado behavior can lead to better lifesaving tornado forecasts. In the 2011 tornado season, more than 550 people lost their lives. It was among the deadliest years on record. Meteorologists are working on new technologies to increase warning time for hurricanes and tornadoes. Their work can potentially save many lives each year.

Other Professional Forecasters

Weather forecasting is not just for storm warnings or telling people what their day will be like. It has many other uses. The military employs meteorologists.

Careers in Monitoring Air Quality

Air quality is a measure of how clean the air is. Air quality monitoring is an important meteorology career. Workers take air samples and perform chemical tests to discover how many pollutants are present. They also look for where pollutants are coming from. They report problems so that actions can be taken to correct them. Governments, companies, and environmental organizations employ air quality monitoring technicians.

They help commanders prepare for troop movements and operations. Naval ships at sea need to know if heavy storms are coming.

Military weather scientists even help the space program. Good weather is needed when launching big rockets. Forecasters track the weather to give approval for liftoff.

Aviation weather forecasting is another meteorology career. Millions of passengers fly from city to city every day. Aviation forecasters gather weather data from around

A military meteorologist takes a weather reading on the ground.

Meteorology professor Robert Pasken demonstrates devices used to study hurricanes.

the world. This helps pilots fly their planes safely and comfortably.

To become meteorologists, students go to college and learn from professors. These professors are usually meteorologists themselves. They teach students the science and math they need to understand weather. They explain how technology helps meteorologists study the atmosphere.

Matt Meister is a meteorologist at a television station in Colorado Springs, Colorado. An interviewer asked him what the most challenging part of his job was:

> *Predicting the future! I have the potential to get egg on my face every day. Occasionally you are going to blow a forecast and you have to be able to recover from that. I do my best to go back and figure out what I missed so that it doesn't happen again. . . .*
>
> *Additionally, I simply can't cover every spot in my viewing area (from the Continental Divide to Kansas and from New Mexico to Denver) for the next seven days in the three minutes I get to present my forecast. I pick the one or two things that [are] most significantly going to affect the most . . . people and call it good. It's about all you can do and be a successful communicator in the television medium.*

Source: "Interview with a Meteorologist." Job Shadow. Job Shadow, 2012. Web. Accessed July 13, 2016.

Consider Your Audience

How would you explain the challenges of being a television meteorologist to another audience, such as your classmates? Write a paragraph about these challenges for the new audience. How does your new text differ from Meister's answer?

CHAPTER FOUR

THE FUTURE OF WEATHER SCIENCE

Meteorology is a promising and exciting career path. The US Department of Labor has predicted that the number of meteorology jobs will increase 9 percent between 2014 and 2024. That's faster than the average growth among all types of jobs.

Private forecasting companies will need experts in weather as it affects agriculture and transportation.

Computers are an important part of any modern meteorologist's job.

Television and radio stations will continue hiring meteorologists as well. Schools and colleges will need meteorology teachers.

Drones and Weather

Some meteorologists are using computer-controlled aircraft, or drones, to study the weather. In the past, most airborne sensors have been attached to balloons. They float along on the wind. Drones can do much more.

One type of drone used in Oklahoma flies near thunderstorms. It soars as high as two miles (3.2 km). It circles the huge cloud formations. Along the way, it

IN THE REAL WORLD

Mega Drones

NASA's enormous Global Hawk drone is 44 feet (13.4 m) long and has a wingspan of 116 feet (35.4 m). It can fly for approximately 9,800 miles (15,800 km). In 2013 NASA sent two Global Hawks far over the Atlantic Ocean to study tropical storms. Both were packed with sensors and equipment. They studied the conditions that cause hurricanes to form.

NASA's weather drones can fly into dangerous weather without putting pilots in harm's way.

measures wind speed, temperature, and pressure. A safety team on the ground spreads out. They make sure piloted aircraft don't come near the drone.

Computers

Computer technology is critical to the future of weather and climate studies. Today, more sensors than ever before are collecting weather data. Satellites in space, drones and balloons in the air, and scientists on the ground are all gathering information. Computers allow meteorologists to make sense of all this data.

Many different factors influence the weather. The more powerful computers become, the more of these factors they can include in their weather models. This results in more accurate forecasts. Computers have made a big difference in just the last few decades. Today's five-day forecasts are approximately as accurate as the one-day forecasts made in the 1970s. Advancing computer technology will continue to push accurate forecasts further into the future.

The *Curiosity* rover contains equipment to measure the temperature and air pressure on Mars.

Weather on Other Planets

Planetary meteorologists study the weather on other

planets. All of the planets in our solar system have

atmospheres. Mercury's atmosphere is extremely thin,

so there is no weather there. Venus's atmosphere is thick and cloudy. It is made up mainly of carbon dioxide. Clouds of sulfuric acid surround the planet and give it a hazy appearance. The atmosphere traps heat, bringing the surface temperature to more than 800 degrees Fahrenheit (427°C). The atmosphere of Mars is mostly carbon dioxide too. However, it is much thinner than Venus's. Winds whip around on the surface and stir up huge dust storms.

Scientists use spacecraft to understand the weather on other worlds. These are often similar to the satellites that study weather on

The Weather on Mars

The first Martian weather forecast came from two spacecraft that landed on the planet's surface. The NASA *Viking 1* and *Viking 2* landers touched down on Mars in 1976. Their main job was to look for signs of life. But they also had equipment to study the weather. Weather instruments measured temperature, air pressure, and winds. The landers discovered the weather changed little from day to day. Major changes happened only between seasons.

	New York City	Mars
High Temperature	42 degrees Fahrenheit (5.6°C)	–9.4 degrees Fahrenheit (–23°C)
Low Temperature	34 degrees Fahrenheit (1.1°C)	–121 degrees Fahrenheit (–85°C)
Air Pressure	10,1829 Pa	854 Pa

Weather on Earth and Mars
This table shows the weather conditions in New York City, New York, and at the location of the *Curiosity* rover on Mars on January 1, 2016. How does Mars differ from Earth? What steps would you need to take to survive on the surface of Mars?

Earth. The spacecraft take images and measure temperatures. In 2015 the *New Horizons* spacecraft collected data about the atmosphere of the distant dwarf planet Pluto. Some spacecraft even land on planets. Several US rovers have landed on Mars and experienced its dust storms firsthand.

Studying the Sky and Saving Lives

On Earth or in outer space, meteorology is an exciting career. Meteorologists use advanced technology to learn all they can about weather. They work to understand one of the most complex systems

Meteorologists are constantly learning more about the fascinating, exciting, and dangerous weather conditions of planet Earth.

imaginable: Earth's atmosphere. This is a tough job, and there is still a long way to go. But weather forecasting is improving all the time. The work of meteorologists expands our knowledge of the planet Earth. It also saves thousands of lives every year.

EXPLORE ONLINE

Chapter Four discusses meteorology in extreme environments, such as the planet Mars. The NASA website below describes weather monitoring instruments on the *Curiosity* rover. *Curiosity* landed on Mars in 2012 and began roving across the Martian surface. It has been sending pictures and data to Earth. This includes weather data. What new information can you learn from the website?

Rover Environmental Monitoring Station (REMS)
mycorelibrary.com/meteorology

FAST FACTS

- Meteorology is the scientific study of the weather and climate of Earth's atmosphere.
- The US Bureau of Labor Statistics estimates that meteorology jobs will increase 9 percent from 2014 to 2024.
- Benjamin Franklin discovered that lightning is electricity. He invented lightning rods to protect buildings from lightning strikes.
- The first known weather instrument was a piece of wool that was hung outside to detect moisture in the air.
- Many new jobs in the meteorology field will be in private weather forecasting companies.
- Private meteorology company jobs focus on the effects of weather on electric power generation, transportation, manufacturing, and agriculture.
- Students can prepare for a meteorology career by studying science, mathematics, and computer science in school.

- Many jobs in meteorology go to broadcast meteorologists who work for TV stations.
- New meteorology tools under development will increase hurricane and tornado warning times and potentially save hundreds of lives each year.
- Scientists have used robotic space probes to study weather on other planets.

STOP AND THINK

Why Do I Care?

Television weather forecasts cover not only local weather but also weather across the country. Why should you care what is happening to the weather elsewhere? Make a list of two or three reasons why knowing about the weather elsewhere might be important.

You Are There

Imagine what it would have been like to be an assistant working for Benjamin Franklin. Ask your school librarian to help you find books on Franklin's weather experiments. Write a letter to your family describing what Franklin and you discovered about weather.

Surprise Me

Chapter Three talks about several careers in the meteorology field. What are a few facts about these careers that you found surprising? Why did you find them surprising?

Take a Stand

Weather satellites can cost hundreds of millions of dollars to build and launch into space. Do you think weather satellites are worth the money spent on them? Write a paragraph explaining your viewpoint.

GLOSSARY

air pressure
the measure of the force exerted by air on the surface of Earth

atmosphere
the layer of air that surrounds Earth

climate
how the weather behaves in a particular location over a long period of time

hurricane
a large, swirling, violent storm

meteorologists
scientists who study Earth's weather and climate

meteorology
the scientific study of Earth's atmosphere

radar
a technology that bounces radio waves or microwaves off of distant objects to figure out their size, location, and direction

tornado
a swirling cloud that forms a funnel shape and causes severe damage as it crosses the land

weather
the condition of the atmosphere, including wind, rain, sunshine, and temperature

LEARN MORE

Books

Furgang, Kathy. *Everything Weather.* Washington, DC: National Geographic, 2012.

Kostigen, Thomas. *Extreme Weather.* Washington, DC: National Geographic, 2014.

Reina, Mary. *The Science of a Hurricane.* Ann Arbor, MI: Cherry Lake Publishing, 2015.

Websites

To learn more about STEM in the Real World, visit **booklinks.abdopublishing.com**. These links are routinely monitored and updated to provide the most current information available.

Visit **mycorelibrary.com** for free additional tools for teachers and students.

INDEX

ABOUT THE AUTHOR

Gregory Vogt is a science educator and children's book author from Houston, Texas. He has written more than 100 books and specializes in helping teachers learn how to teach science.